The Little Book of Daytime Illusions

"two and through"

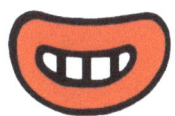

by Kevin James

An ode to nature and ideas.

The Little Book of Daytime Illusions is brought to you by The Fuchsian Gallery Co., the fusion between colors and ideas. Thank you for viewing.

Please take advantage of the free pages inside of this book. Create with me. Let the illustrations take your imagination down a whimsical journey.

- Kevin James

The Deep:

Mysteries of the Ocean

The ocean, at first glance, is one of the most breathtaking sites that one could experience at any point of their lives. What mysteries that the ocean holds could host a conversation for hours, I know. For now, let's enjoy the vibe of being one with sea.

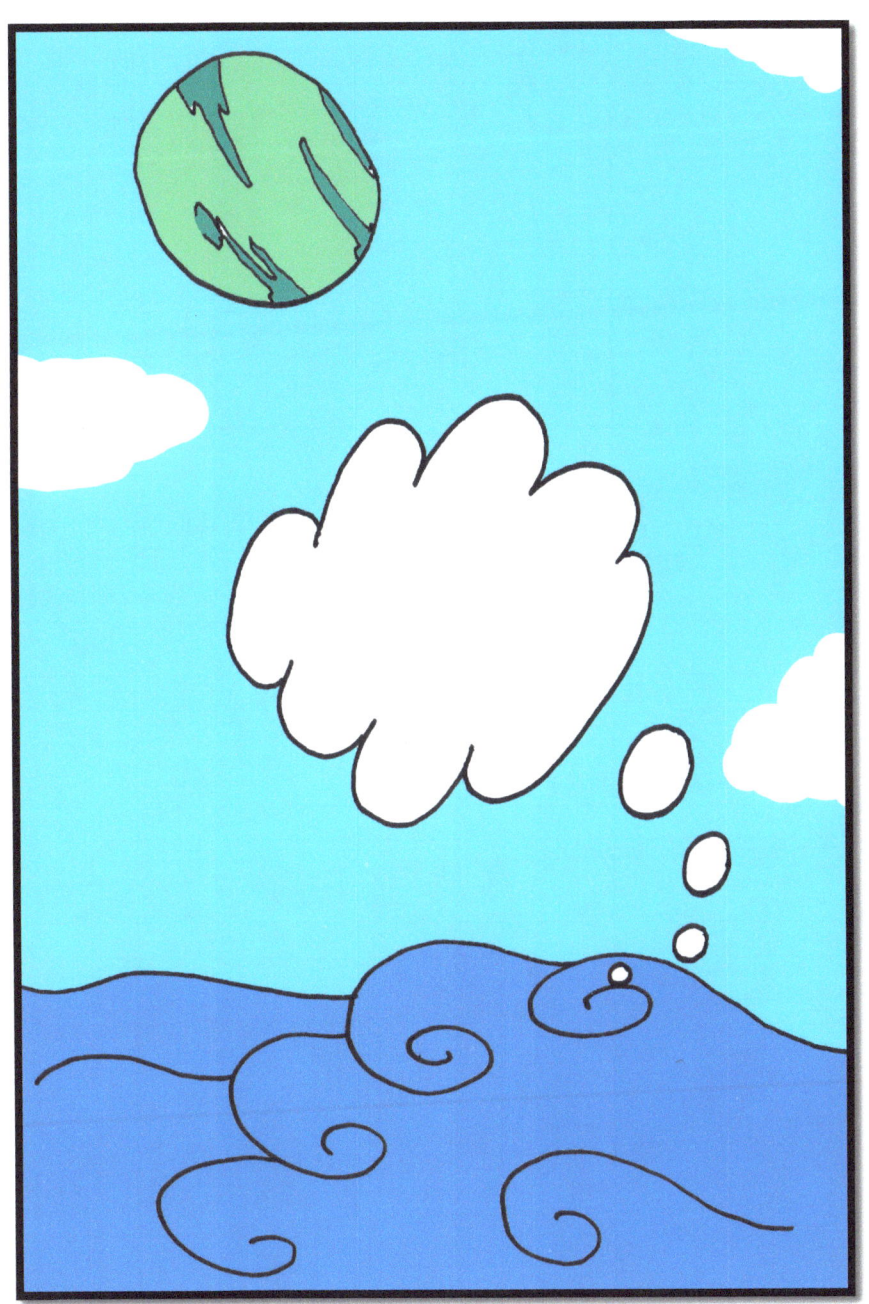

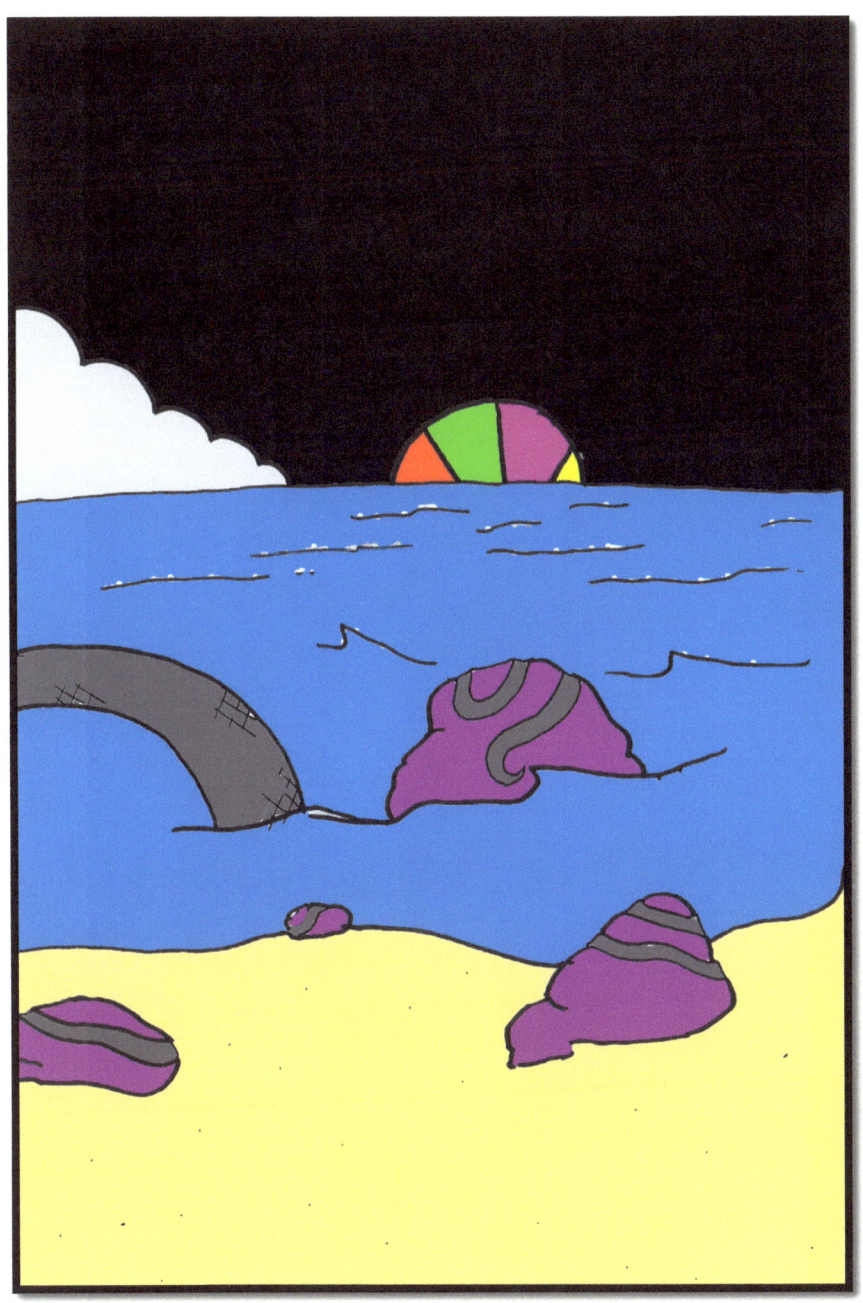

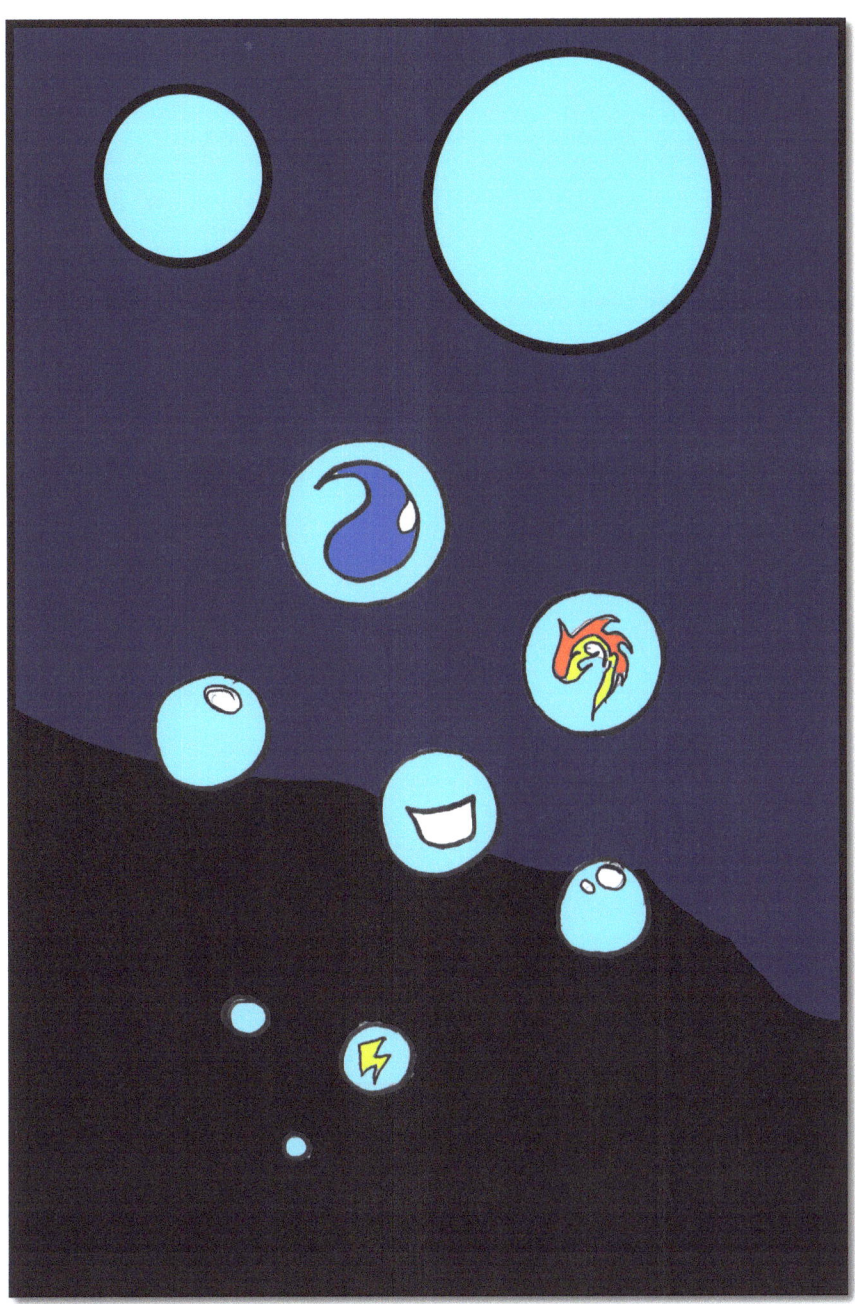

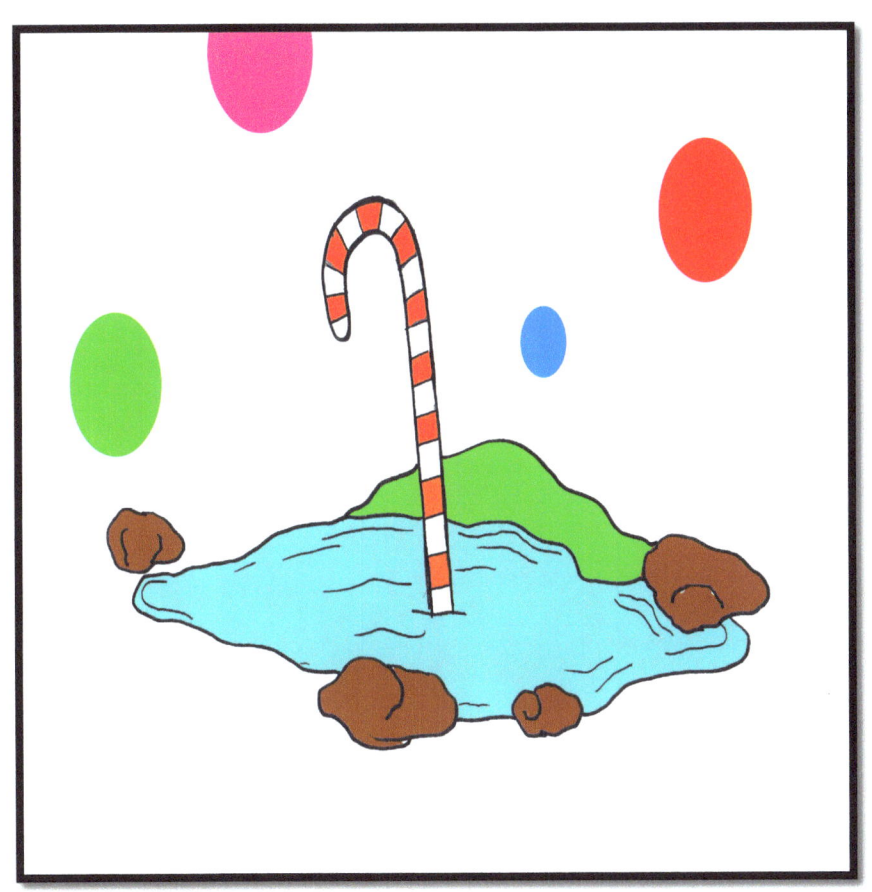

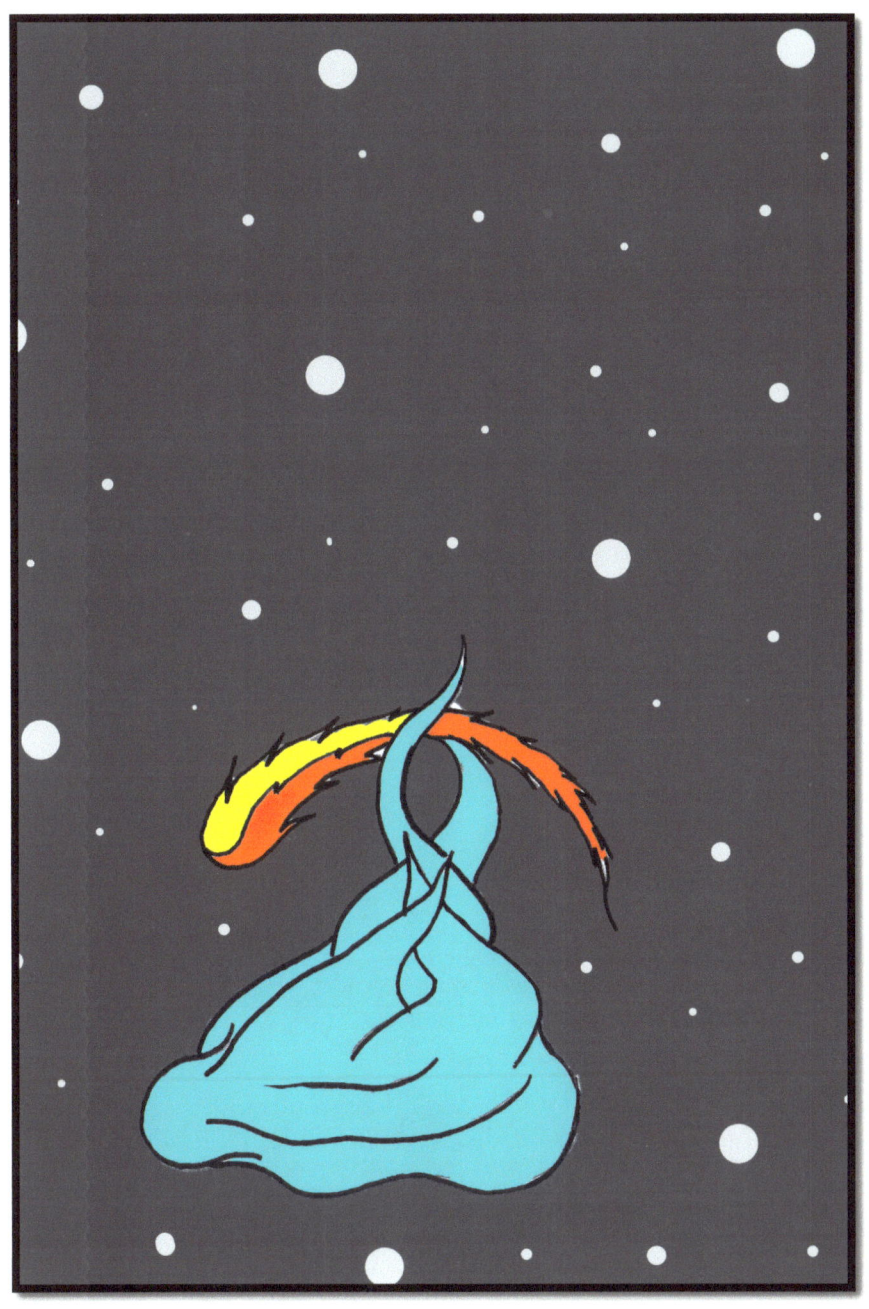

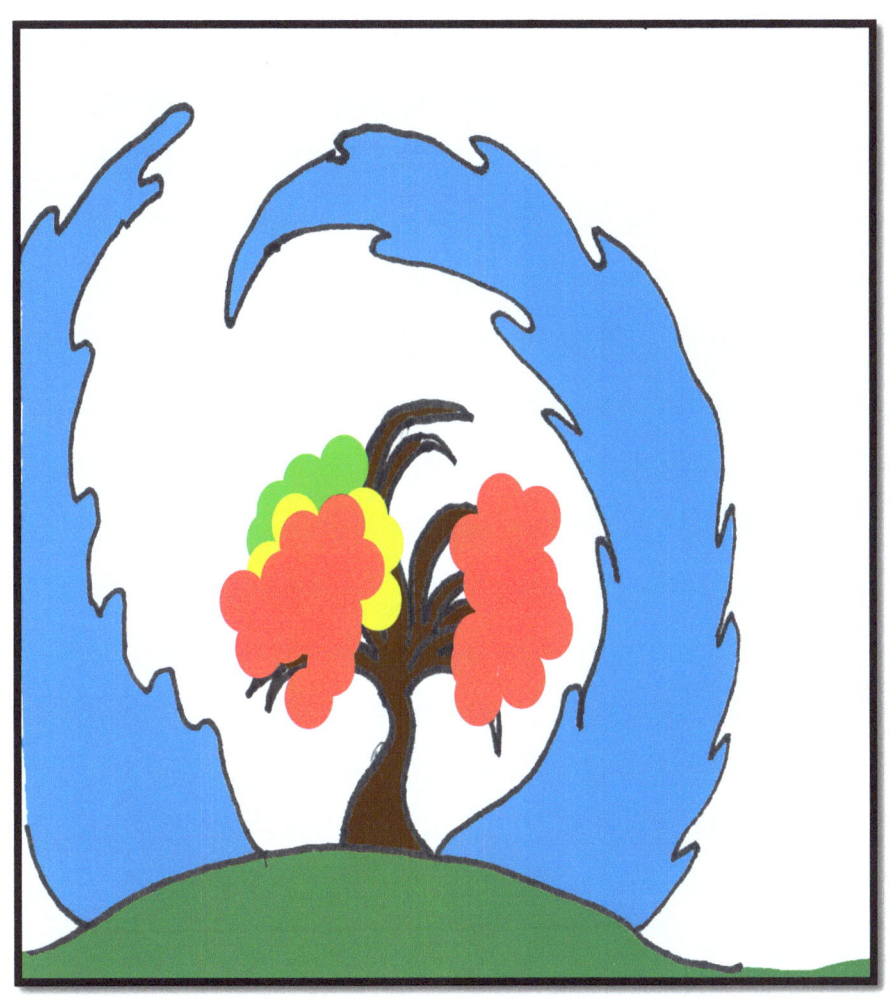

Up In Space:

THE UNIVERSE

When you look into the night sky, what comes to your thoughts? Do you think about life elsewhere in the galaxy, extraterrestrials coming to earth, or going out there to explore space on your own? You're not alone. The universe is undoubtedly evolving at a rapid speed at this current second. It's given us humans much to work on and wonder about.

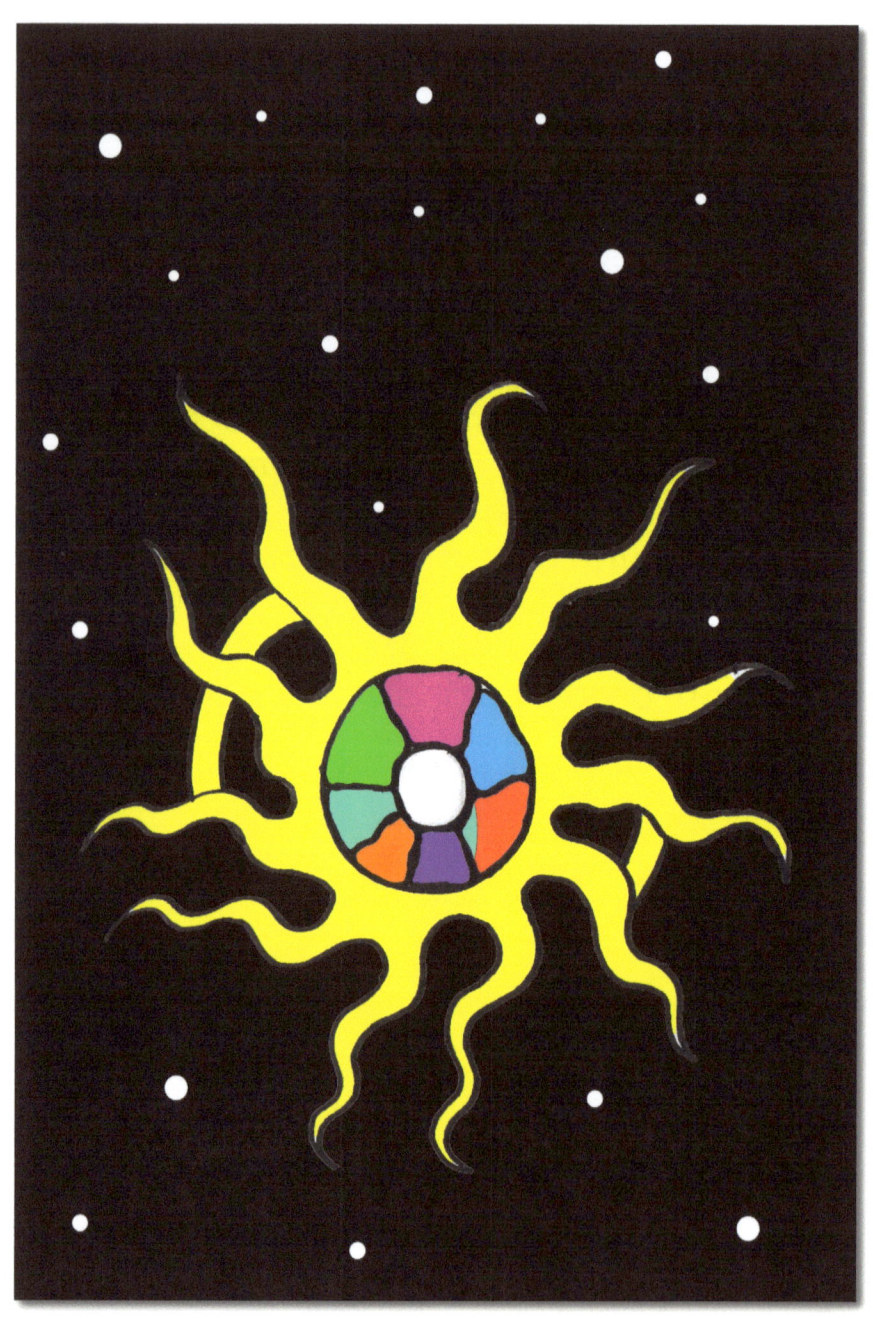

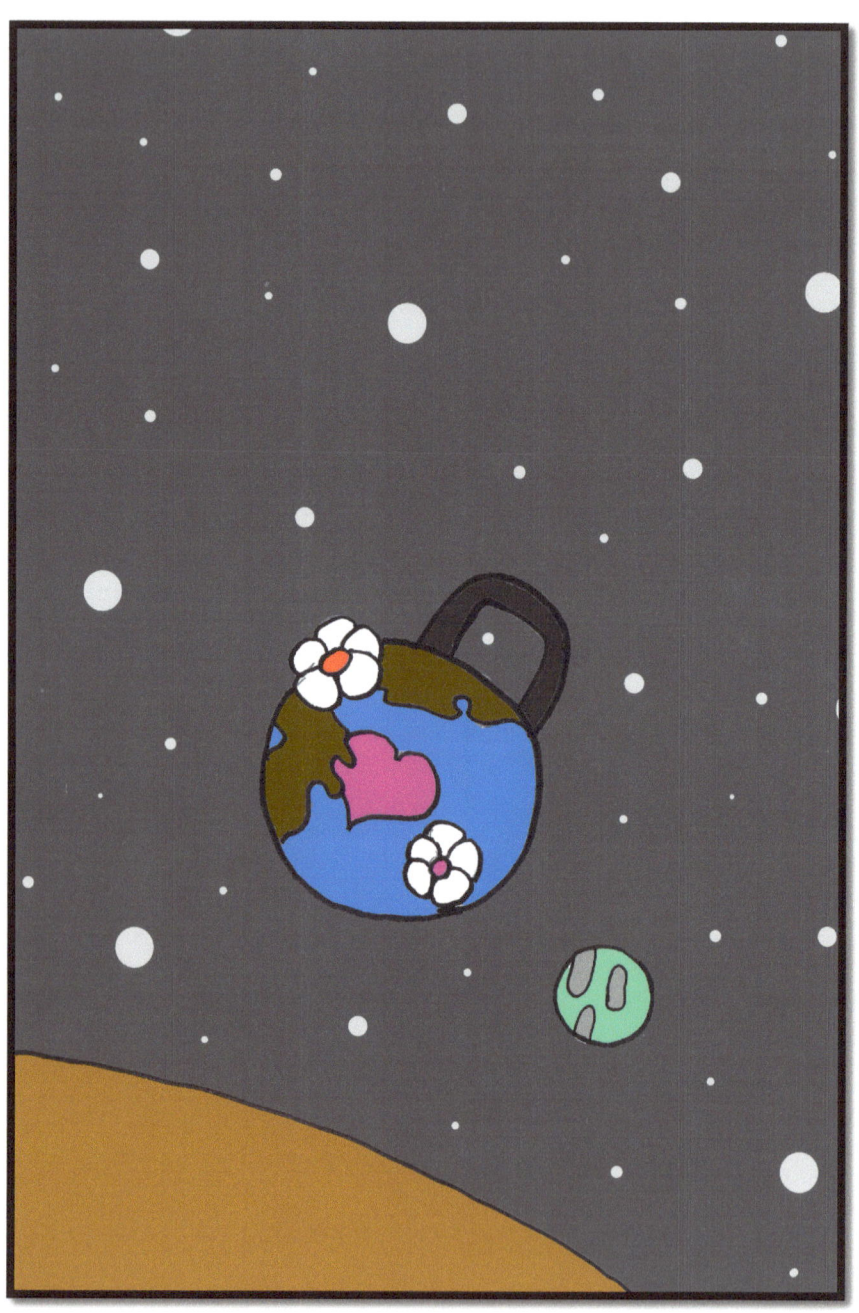

The Earth:

FLOWER POWER

Apart from space, the earth holds it's own mysteries other than just below the water. The beautiful, regenerating plant is also something to adore and give a little thought. A plant is able to live through harsh conditions and yet, survive to see another day, completely restored. Trees not only make for great childhood stories, but also, trees provide us with oxygen to live and thrive. It's time to see the power of the flower through the imagination!

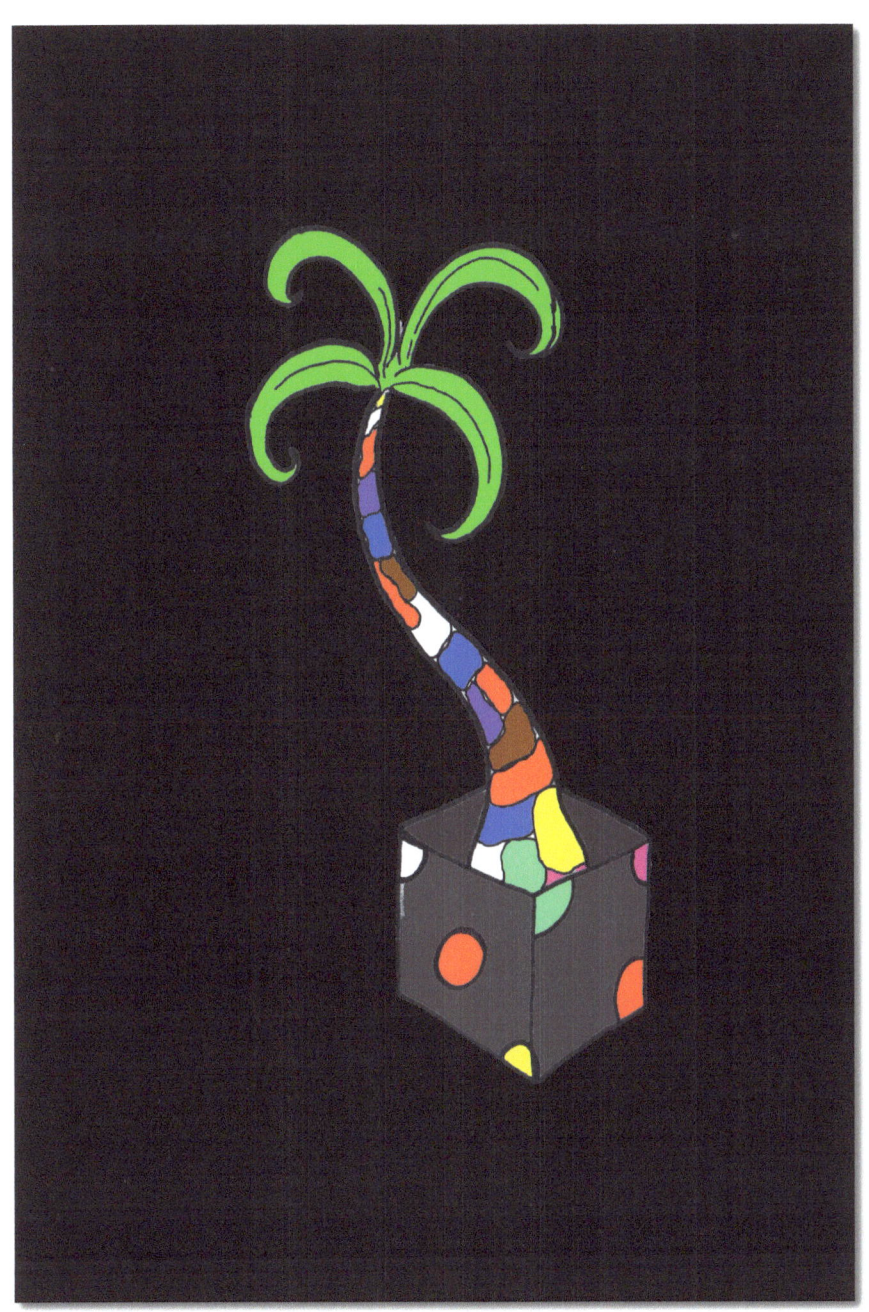

On this work, that blue spot is dried paint
which accidentally got on the work. I
thought it would give the illustration
"character".

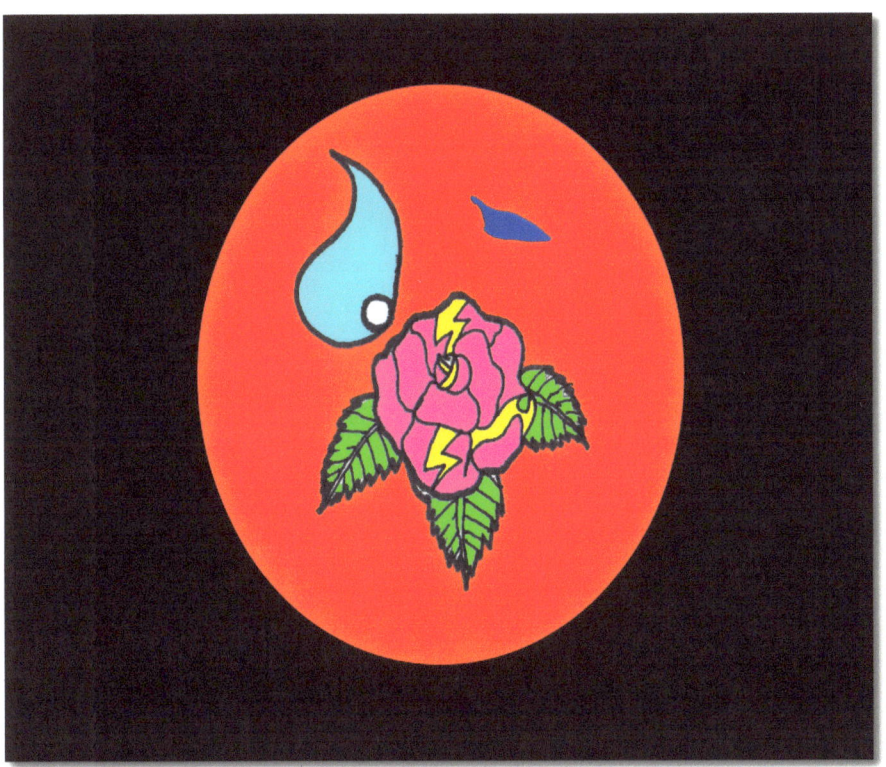

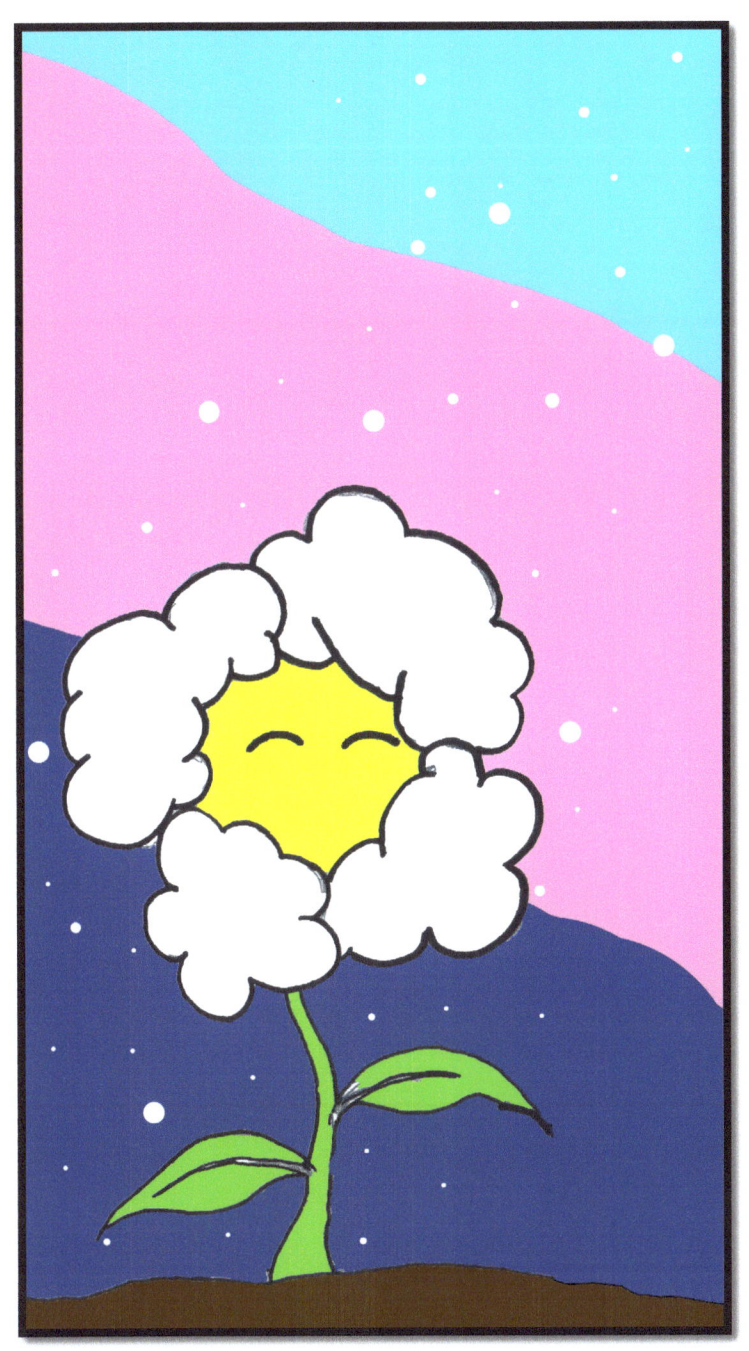

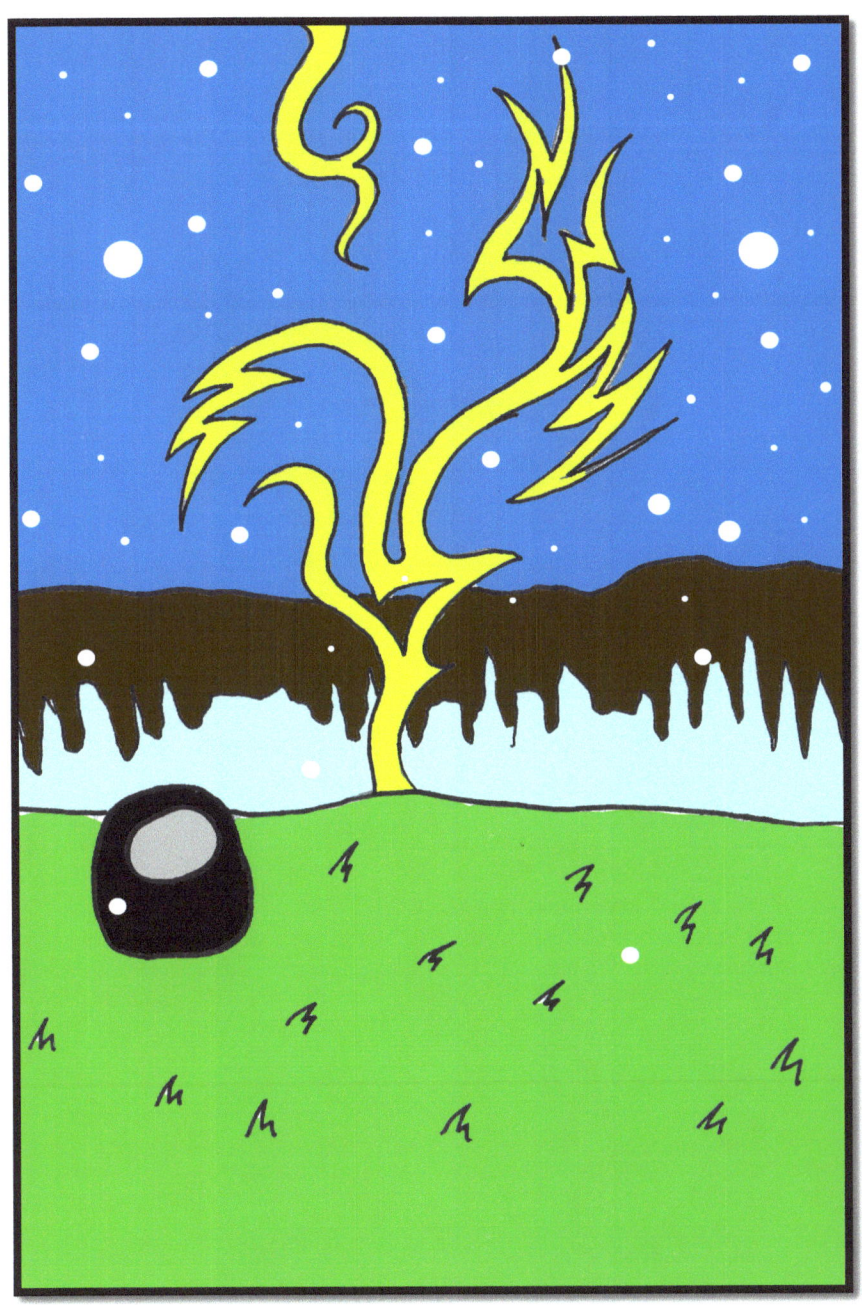

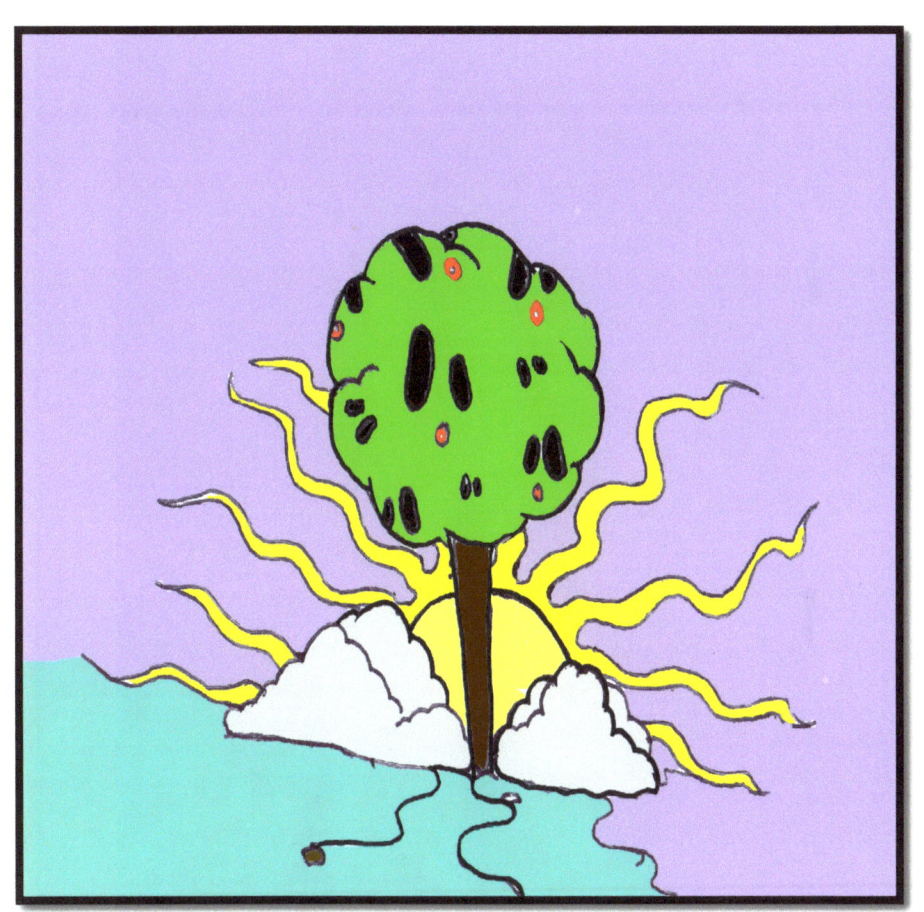

The Highest Point:

THE MOUNTAINS

How high are you willing to travel up the highest mountain in your region? The climb is usually very high, which is what makes mountains so unique and breathtaking. We have thought about the mysteries of the deep, now let's think higher.

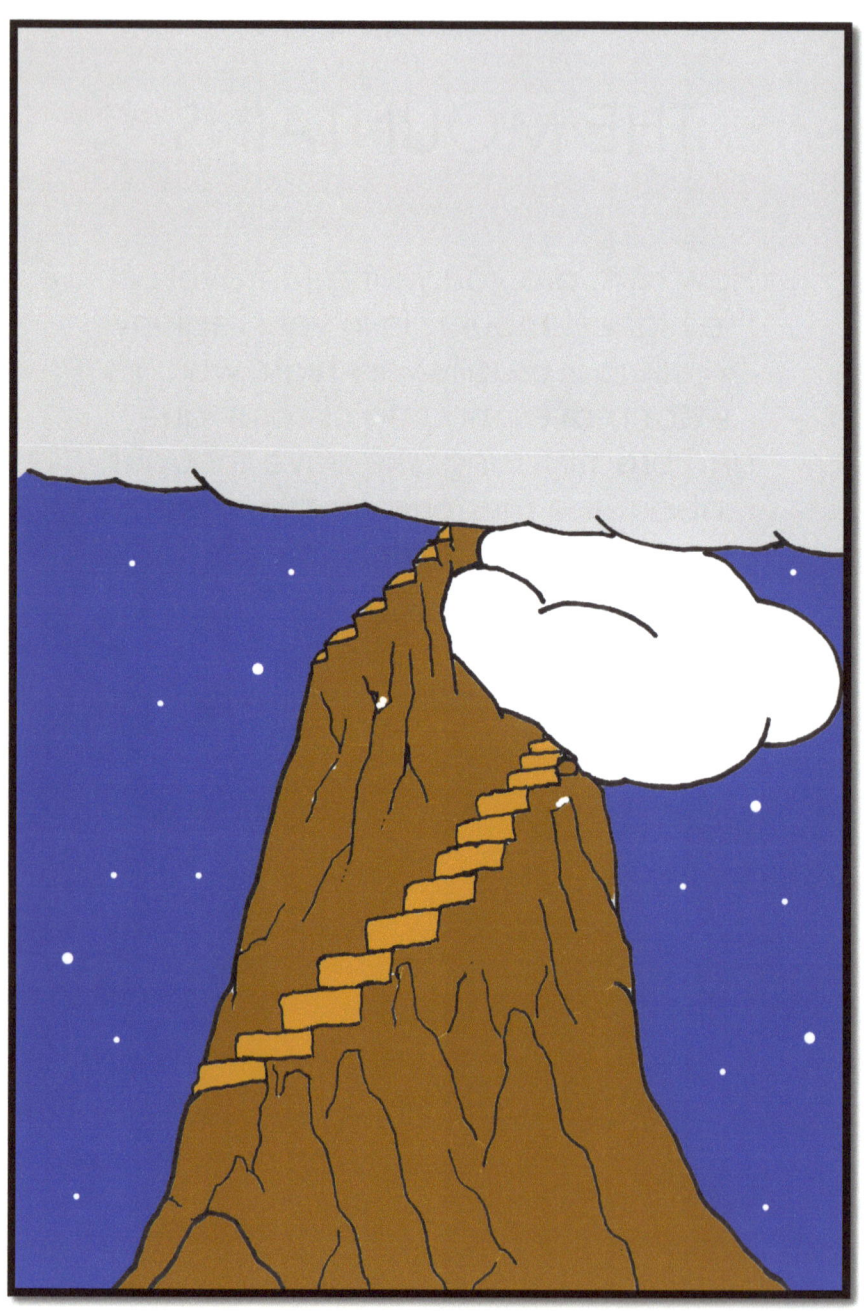

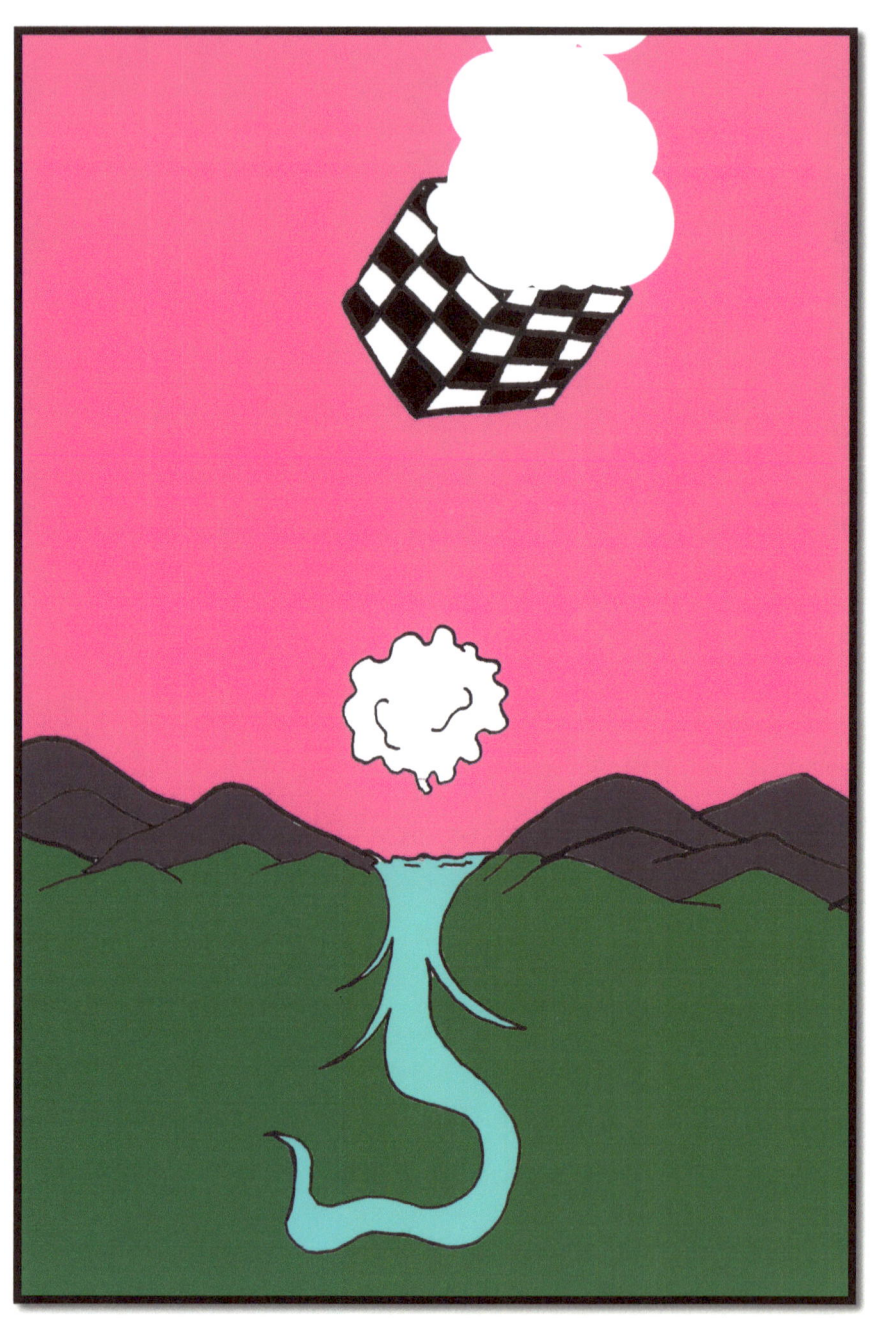

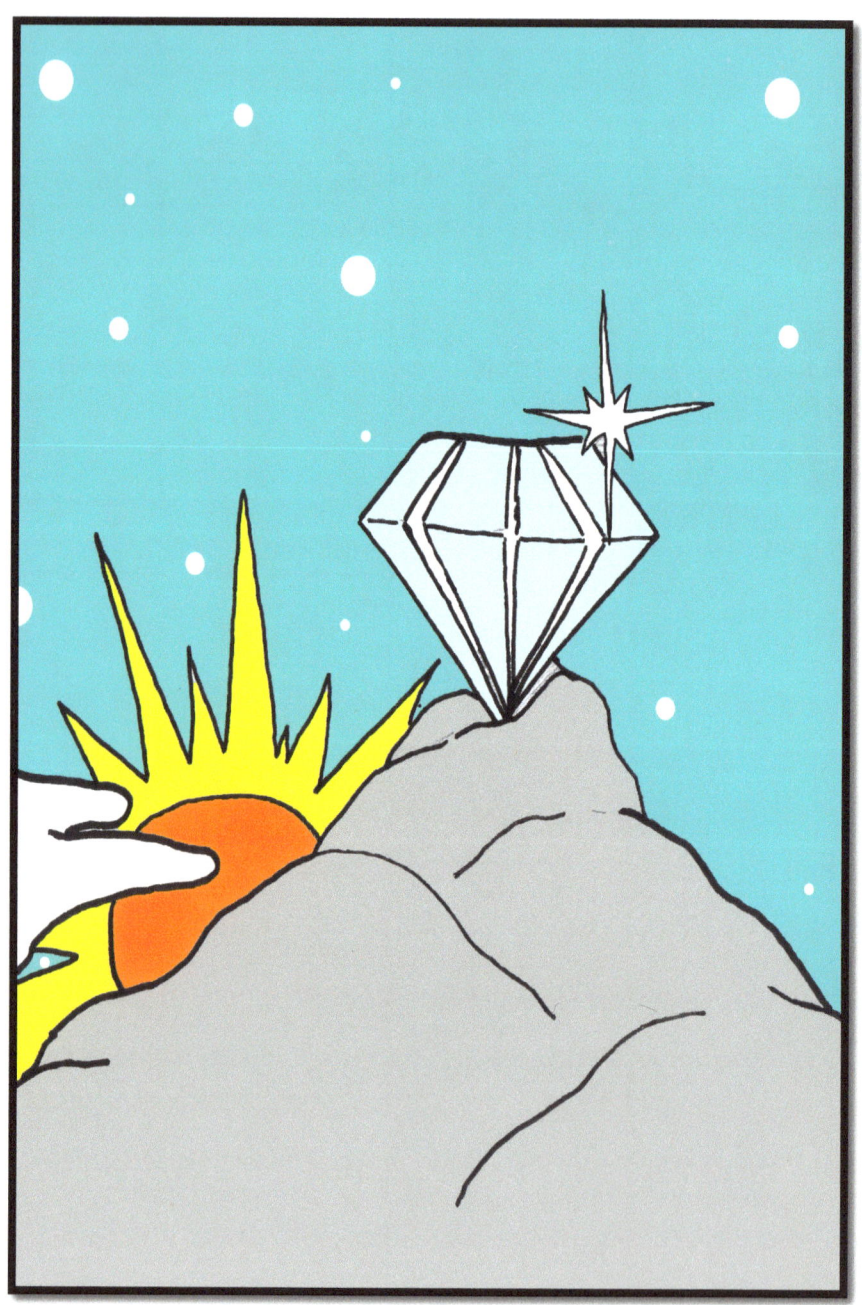

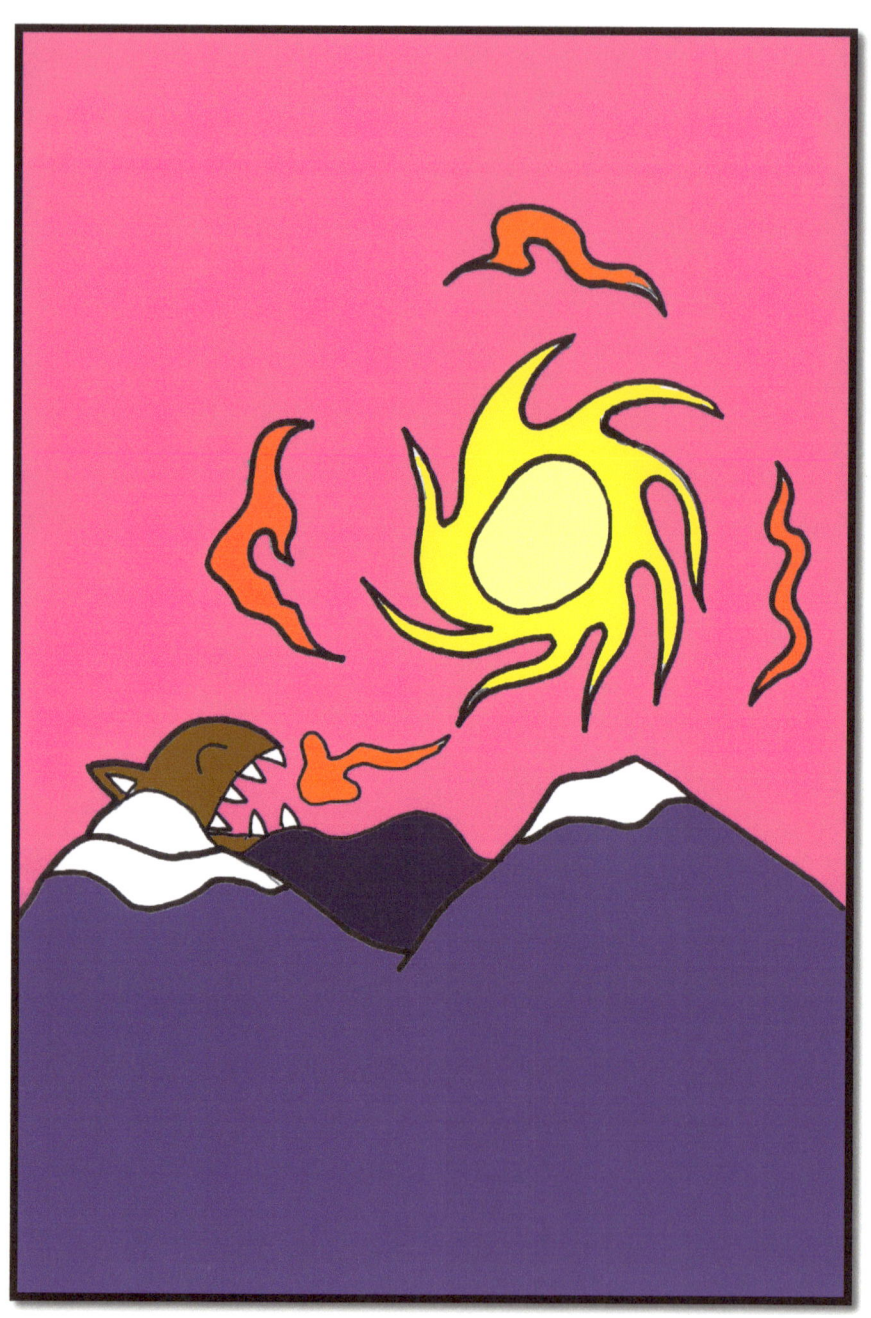

The Life:

THE IMAGINATION

Guess what else is a breathtaking part of nature? The human mind is. Our imaginations have produced telescopes capable of seeing what the universe has to offer. Our imaginations have us flying 30,000 feet over the surface of the earth while being served hot tea in a comfortable chair. I haven't begun to name what the human mind has given to all of us. Just know this, if you knew what YOU were truly capable of, you would astound yourself.

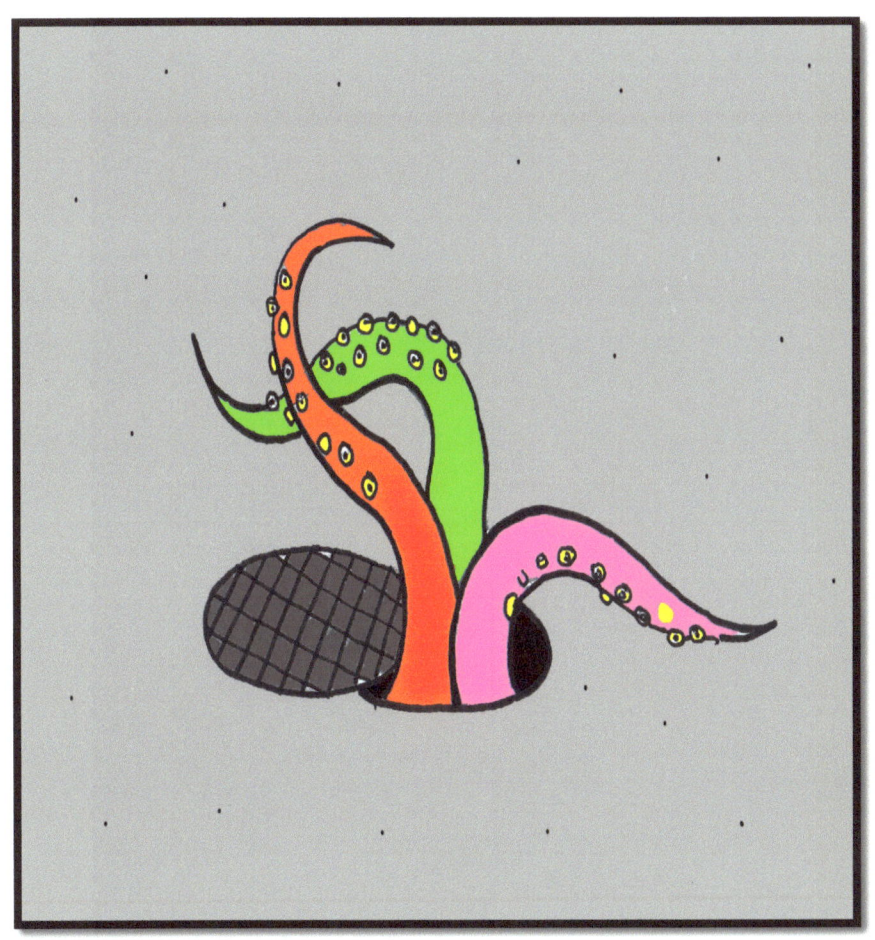

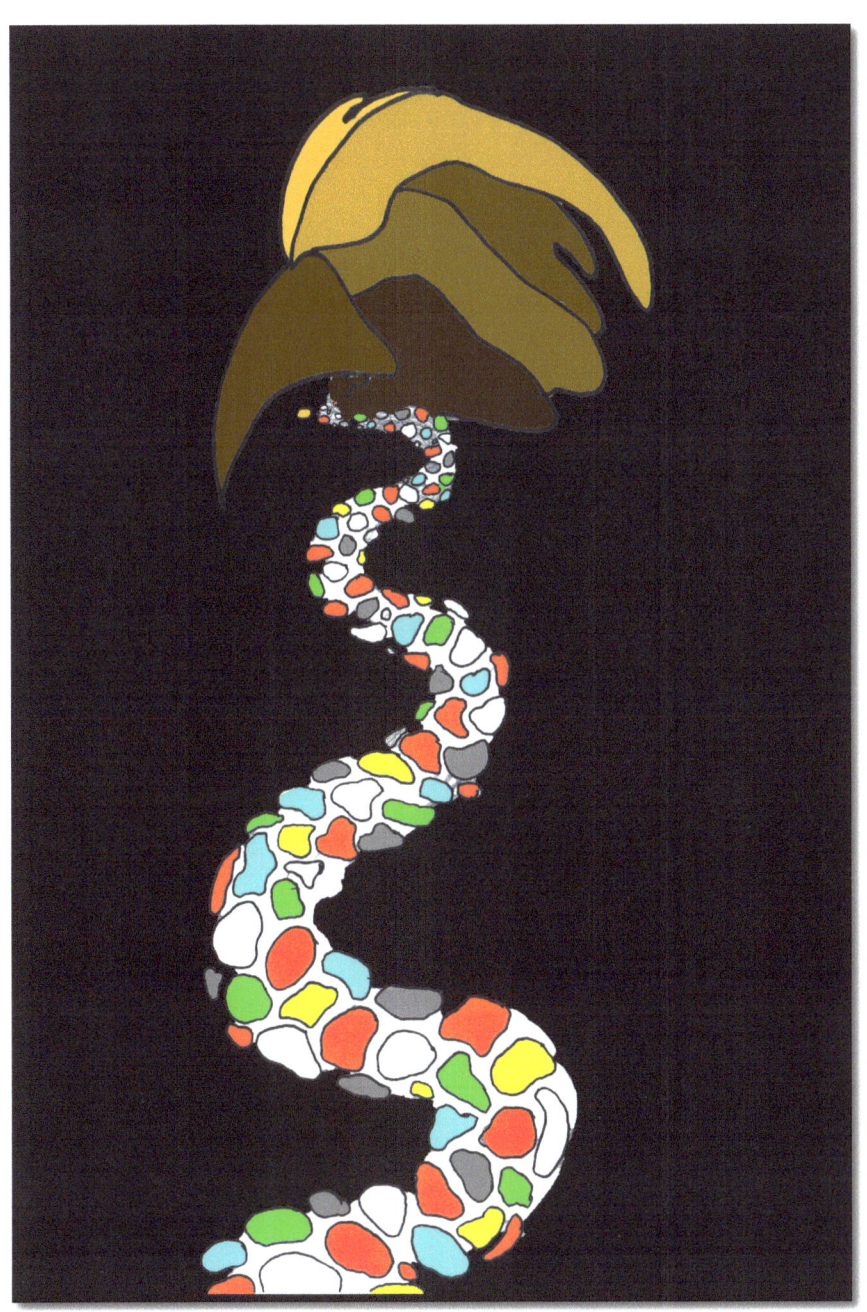

This is the end of The Little Book of Daytime Illusions journey. I hope that this book series has inspired you to take creative action. All that it takes is to see the world from a different perspective.

Thank you.

Now available from The Fuchsian Gallery Company on Kindle and all digital bookstores.

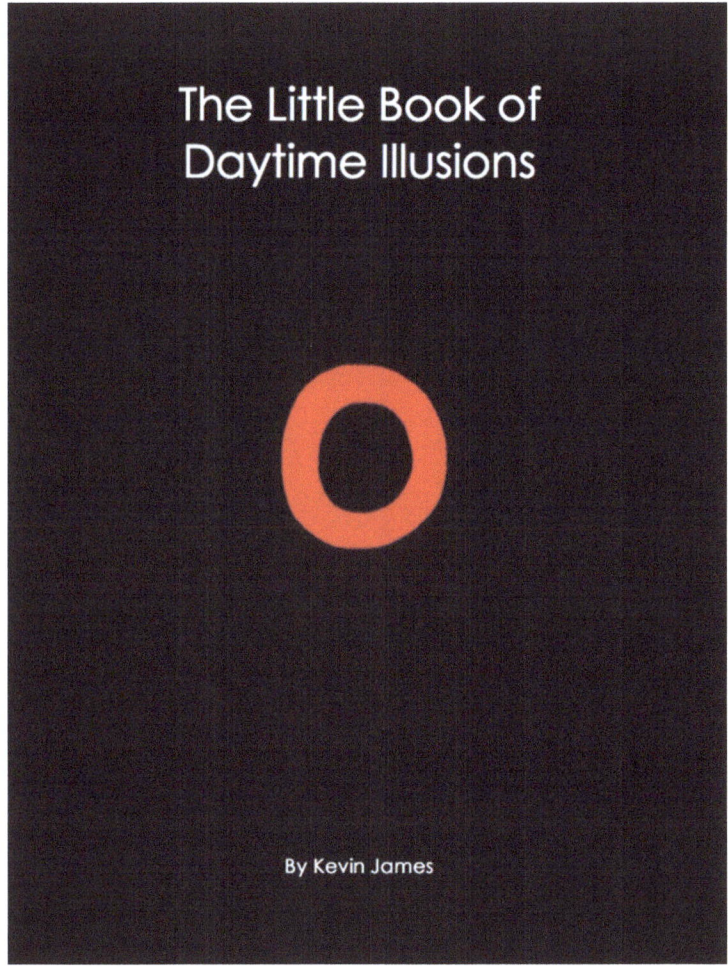

the fuchsian gallery company

from Kevin James

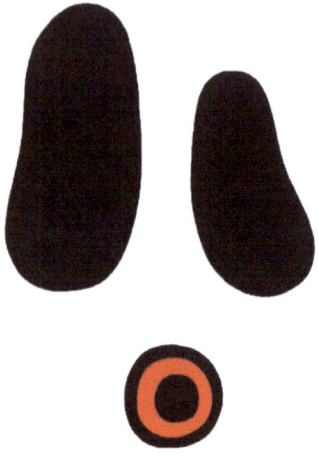

2016